WHO ARE THE BRETHREN
AND DOES IT MATTER?

Who are the Brethren and does it matter?

HAROLD H. ROWDON

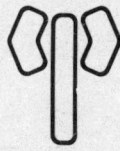

published on behalf of
CHRISTIAN BRETHREN RESEARCH FELLOWSHIP

Exeter
The Paternoster Press

AUSTRALIA:
*Bookhouse Australia Ltd.,
P.O. Box 115, Flemington Markets, NSW 2129*

SOUTH AFRICA:
*Oxford University Press,
P.O. Box 1141, Cape Town*

British Library Cataloguing in Publication Data

Rowdon, Harold H.
 Who are the Brethren and does it matter?
 1.Brethren
 I.Title
 289.9   BX8800

ISBN 0-85364-398-9

Typeset in Great Britain by
Photoprint, 9–11 Alexandra Lane, Torquay, Devon
and printed for The Paternoster Press,
Paternoster House, 3 Mount Radford Crescent, Exeter, Devon
by Maslands Ltd., 16a Fore Street, Tiverton, Devon.

CONTENTS

Adapted from articles in
HARVESTER, April to July, 1985

1
AN IDENTITY CRISIS?

There was a time when it was not difficult to define the term 'Brethren' ('Open' variety). For the most part they believed and practised the same things, and those beliefs and practices were highly distinctive. Unlike almost all other groups of Christians they managed without full-time workers resident in a particular locality, the breaking of bread accompanied by open worship was their major corporate activity, their main evangelistic thrust was a gospel meeting each Sunday evening (supplemented by occasional missions lasting for a week or more) and their chief teaching method was a regular conversational Bible reading, held on a weeknight. Their theology was dispensationalist, with an almost universal belief in the pre-tribulation rapture of the church prior to the return of Christ in glory with his church to set up his earthly kingdom. On the whole they worked in isolation from other Christians, many being led to believe that there were few, if any, fully committed Christians in 'the denominations'. They maintained a fairly rigid view of separation from the world in terms of minimal contact with society.

As will be urged later, this is something of an over-simplification. But not seriously so. Individuals and assemblies which were regarded as deviationalist

were treated as such. The faithful would be duly
warned against them.

Furthermore, though the concept of the autonomy
of the local assembly was jealously guarded, close
links were forged between individuals and assemblies
throughout the country. The Westminster Missionary
Meetings in London served one of the functions of a
denominational 'assembly' by bringing together Brethren from all over the country for social as well as
religious purposes and thus helping to create a sense of
solidarity. Virtually all the missionaries who went
abroad from assemblies did so in fellowship with the
editors of *Echoes of Service* and were linked together
with the individuals and assemblies that supported
them by means of a well thought out support system.

Group solidarity was further strengthened by means
of the magazines which circulated widely among
assemblies (and very rarely beyond them, I would
judge). The uniformity of their teaching helped materi-
ally to create a common body of beliefs and practices.
This was strongly reinforced by the system of 'conferences'. Most of these were arranged by particular
assemblies for the benefit of their own attenders, but
all other assemblies in the area were warmly invited—
and expected—to attend *en masse*. It was probably
quite common for Brethren in earlier days to spend a
large number of Saturday afternoons and evenings
each year attending the local round of conferences.
Some conferences were more ambitious, lasting for
several days and attracting attenders from considerable distances. In his youth, my father used to cycle
from Lyndhurst in Hampshire to Yeovil in Somerset
for the annual conference (which, by the way, continued to be held until a few years ago).

Another way by which assemblies safeguarded their
identity was the use of visiting speakers. Some of these

worked full-time at it, going from place to place for a week or a fortnight of special teaching meetings. Most were in 'secular' employment, but devoted many Saturdays in the course of a year, as well as most Sunday evenings, to speaking at conferences and other types of meeting. A few of them expressed 'eccentric' ideas, but the majority reinforced the held beliefs of older people and introduced younger folk to standard Brethren beliefs.

In those days, people knew what Brethren stood for, and Brethren themselves knew it even better! Today that has largely gone. More and more Brethren are availing themselves of the freedom they had always claimed to possess of testing their beliefs and practices by the touchstone of Scripture. As a result, some are modifying their beliefs if these are felt to be unwarranted or mistaken, and are adapting their practices where these are felt to need modification in the light of changed conditions—provided that such adaptation would not be in conflict with the clear teaching of Scripture.

The traditional mould which gave shape and form to the Brethren movement has been broken, and this has enabled a rich diversity to become apparent which, incidentally, is in greater harmony with New Testament teaching and practice. But it has created a Brethren identity crisis. Do Brethren churches which have recovered the freedom to be biblical forfeit the label 'Brethren'? Do they wish to retain it? Is there any point in perpetuating it? Are they anything other than local churches seeking to apply biblical principles to church life in the late twentieth century?

The issue has been sharpened by the fact that these changes have taken place concurrently with others that have occurred in non-Brethren churches.

What has happened is that a small but growing

number of churches standing right outside the Brethren movement have adopted a number of the once distinctive hallmarks of Brethren identity. Shared leadership, open worship—often associated with breaking of bread—and clear evangelistic preaching on a regular basis are cases in point. Sadly it has to be admitted that there is little evidence that these things have been learned from those of us who are Brethren. Gladly we acknowledge that they have learned them from a common source—Scripture.

So, more and more Anglican churches are developing team ministries using not only full-time men and women but also lay readers and lay pastors who share in the preaching, teaching and pastoral care of the church. They may also include periods of open worship in their services. Even their traditional practice of baptizing infants is coming under question and, increasingly, is being superseded by a form of dedication which differs very little from the thanksgiving for a newly born child which is offered in many Brethren churches.

Again, an increasing number of Baptist churches are appointing elders to assist the minister in pastoral care, and some of them make provision for open worship, often in the context of the breaking of bread. There never was more than a hairbreadth between a certain type of Baptist church and a certain type of Brethren church. Now the hair has been split!

Does it matter?

But does it matter?, someone is bound to ask. Is it not better to leave the rough edges indeterminate rather than attempt to define them precisely? To do so, it is arguable, would be to distinguish between Brethren and other churches in a way that is sectarian.

Curiously, this kind of argument can be heard coming from both ends of the Brethren spectrum. At the more traditional end, where there is considerable reluctance to change received ideas and practices, the argument runs something like this. Those called by others 'Brethren' are in fact nothing more than Christians. They never wanted any distinctive label other than this. They wish to say or do nothing which would distinguish them from other Christians.

But those who argue like this do not seem to realize that concealed within this line of argument is the implication that they alone meet on valid Christian ground (i.e. non-sectarian ground) and that other Christians *ought* to be meeting with them. Their objection to admitting a distinctive Brethren identity would therefore seem to arise from an unwillingness to admit that the Brethren position is one of a number of more or less acceptable alternatives. It stands alone. Ironically, this is in fact a classic example of sectarian thinking!

The reluctance of those at the opposite end of the Brethren spectrum (the open-minded end which is committed not to perpetuating a received tradition for its own sake but to applying the teaching of Scripture to changing conditions, trusting in the guidance of the Holy Spirit) to acknowledge any kind of Brethren identity arises from almost opposite considerations.

They have a deep and understandable anxiety not to be confused with the Exclusive Brethren who in recent years have attracted such adverse attention and, indeed, have forfeited the sympathy of all right-thinking people. The term 'Brethren' has become a loaded one, evoking prejudice and misunderstanding. The task of explaining the difference between 'Exclusive' and 'Open' Brethren is difficult, and it may seem easier and more effective to jettison the term.

By the same token, many of the more open-minded Brethren are reluctant to run the risk of being associated with those traditional Open Brethren whose legalistic spirit, rigidity and formality seem to them to run contrary to the letter and the spirit of the New Testament.

Possibly of even greater importance is the fear that any kind of tie with other Brethren—even those of like mind—will prejudice relationships with their non-Brethren fellow-Christians. Not for them any emphasis on the things that they share in common with other Brethren, if that has the effect of diverting attention from their ties with other Christians who do not happen to belong to the same ecclesiastical tradition. They are rather like those in Corinth who disavowed being followers of men like Paul, Apollos or Cephas, but claimed to be followers of Christ (*1 Cor. 1:12*)!

How it all came about

Mention has already been made of the Exclusive Brethren, and there can be no doubt that one factor in inducing the current identity crisis among Brethren has been the publicity given to the name as a result of the tragic developments within the Exclusives during the past few decades. It was some time before the media became aware of the distinction between Exclusive and Open Brethren. The term 'Brethren' became associated with crack-pot regulations, ostracism of non-conforming relatives, broken marriages and broken homes, inhumanity and even suicide.

Eventually the media mostly realized that the Exclusives had broken off all relationships with their Open counterparts nearly a century and a half ago, and constituted a distinct and separate entity. But the damage had been done. The name of Brethren had been tarnished. It had acquired overtones which made it embarrassing. Any attempt to dissociate it from those overtones calls for close scrutiny of Brethren identity.

Meanwhile something else had been happening which was to cause long and hard thinking about the same subject. At least since the second world war, a steady drift away from Brethren churches had been taking place. Men called up for military service during and immediately after the war, and students going away to college as a result of the boom in higher education during the post-war years, discovered that there were genuine Christians in non-Brethren churches. In many cases they had been taught that other churches were apostate, or at least riddled with modernism, and that true Christianity was all but non-existent outside Brethren churches.

Not only did they discover that this was not so, but they also found fellowship in non-Brethren churches where the gospel was faithfully preached, the Word of God taught with a power and authority beyond anything they had known before, and the people of God cared for pastorally in a way to which they had not been accustomed. (Of course this was not the experience of all, but it happened often enough to be significant.)

The process continued, if only because the 'sixties witnessed a degree of spiritual revival in (usually) Anglican churches which was running parallel with a decline of spiritual life and vigour in some Brethren churches. A little later, the beginnings of similar revival in Baptist (and some other) churches ante-dated the spiritual stirrings which we are beginning to experience in a number of Brethren churches.

There were other reasons for the spiritual 'brain drain' of indeterminate but probably substantial pro-

portions which took place. The intransigence of the
leadership in some of the churches that possessed
leadership; the suspicion (and sometimes the jealousy)
shown towards 'angry young men'; the terrible incubus
resulting from minority rule (otherwise known as the
principle of not taking a decision without unanimity);
and the reluctance of some dominant Brethren to take
seriously the aspirations, and even the undoubted
spiritual gifts of younger people: these are some of
them.

That those who made the transition from Brethren
to other types of evangelical church were not all
worthless malcontents is shown by the number of
highly respected ministers of churches—Anglican as
well as Free Church—and deacons of Baptist and
Independent Free churches who acknowledge (almost
always without bitterness and often with nostalgia)
their Brethren roots.

It was during the same post-war period that Open
Brethren began to show signs of moving away from
what is technically known as a 'sect' mentality to a
'denominational' stance. This can be seen in a number
of ways. Some churches began to replace their 'tin
tabernacles' with buildings of brick or stone. Instead of
being called 'Hall', these meeting places were dubbed
'Chapel' or 'Evangelical Church'. Rather than holding
'meetings' at which 'addresses' were given by 'speakers',
they arranged 'services' during which 'sermons' were
delivered by 'preachers'. Almost without realizing it,
they were taking their place as one of a range of
denominational options instead of assuming a position
of solitary splendour with their own style of architec-
ture, nomenclature and procedure, as if theirs was the
only valid Christian presence which, therefore, should
be seen to be different in as many ways as possible.

Also during this period, movements, activities and

publishing events were taking place which highlighted the question of Brethren identity.

A private conference, held in a London hotel in 1953, probed into the contentious issue of the study of prophecy, and showed that controversial matters could be debated in an atmosphere of mutual acceptance and understanding—even though differences of opinion remained! It was followed by a similar conference on the Holy Spirit, and the still-running series of more open conferences held first at High Leigh and then at Swanwick. These probed deeply into the ecclesiastical, doctrinal and ethical perspectives of Brethren thinking, though their impact on local church life was somewhat limited.

Perhaps the most significant of these conferences— for our present purpose—was the one held in 1978, with its report published in 1979 under the title *Where do we go from here?* This revealed willingness on the part of some well-known ministers of the Word to question the validity of Brethren going into the later decades of the twentieth century with methods unchanged and problems unexamined. Hostile reviews in the more conservative Brethren magazines pointed up the polarization to which we will turn presently and which proves to the hilt that there *is* a Brethren identity crisis.

But first we must look at the foundation of the Christian Brethren Research Fellowship (1963) and the publication of *A New Testament Commentary for Today* (1969) and *A Bible Commentary for Today* (1979). CBRF provided a rallying-point for those men and women who are committed to Brethren churches but sit relatively loose to Brethren traditions *as such*. The commentaries showed that, despite their losses to other churches, the Brethren still included among their number those who were acquainted with the biblical languages and possessed the gift of biblical exegesis. For some, they restored confidence in the movement. For others, they showed that traditional interpretations of Scripture were losing their popularity, since they were not particularly stressed in the commentaries and were sometimes conspicuous by their absence. A vigorous 'conservative backlash' followed. CBRF became a 'dirty' term in some quarters. The commentaries received hostile reviews. Young people were sternly cautioned against the 'foe within' as well as those 'without'. Nor was it easy for less traditional Brethren to speak well of their more traditional counterparts.

Polarization is nothing new among Brethren. For that matter, every movement tends to have left and right wings! The bitter controversies of earlier days are best forgotten—except as warnings against going that way again. For if one thing is clear about the Brethren scene today it is the fact of polarization. You can see it in the range of magazines published for the same constituency. It shows itself in sharply contrasting styles of Bible exposition. It may be discerned in the alternative conferences that are available with their almost entirely different choice of speakers. In some areas there are even options in youth rallies! But for the absence of formal connexionalism and the measure of grace exercised on both sides there would surely have been some kind of open rift by now.

As a result of the freedom which some Brethren churches feel able to exercise in good conscience, a further complicating factor has arisen. The application of biblical principles to life in the contemporary world has caused some churches to appear to step out of line. For example, realizing that Sunday evening is one of the worst times in the week for effective evangelism, an increasing number of churches have opted for

Sunday morning family services instead of the traditional Sunday evening gospel meetings. Sometimes this has resulted in a Sunday evening communion service (not an apparently unbiblical practice on the face of it!). Again, faced with a grave lack of pastoral care and/or time for biblical study and teaching, some churches have opted for the use of resident full-time workers (by no means an unknown practice abroad, though not so common in this country) in a serious effort to provide adequate spiritual care and food for God's people without compromise of biblical teaching. An even more dramatic example is the fact that, alerted by current trends, an increasing number of churches have gone back to Scripture to see if they have correctly understood its teaching on matters such as the role of women in the church and the range of spiritual gifts given today. As a result they have sometimes felt it right to amend traditional practices. Sometimes the changes have been of such magnitude as to cause more traditional Brethren churches to distance themselves (a far cry from the disavowal of any kind of Brethren identity!). For their part, the churches that have made such changes have sometimes played down their Brethren connections, even to the point of denying that they exist!

Finally—and importantly—is the fact, already noted, that more and more churches outside the Brethren movement are embracing beliefs and practices that used to be regarded as distinctively Brethren. If it is hard to give reasons why some churches are known as Brethren, it is almost as hard to know why others are not!

It should be clear by now that there is an identity crisis of considerable proportions. Many are embarrassed by the term, Brethren. Some have become disillusioned with traditional forms of Brethren church

life and have either moved elsewhere or modified the
supposedly sacrosanct pattern. In response, others
have set their faces against change and reiterate the
old shibboleths, while of those who have changed,
some have carried the process so far as to raise the
question whether the term, Brethren, is appropriate to
them—assuming that they wish to be known as such!
Meanwhile, churches from other traditions have taken
on some of the most distinctive features of a Brethren
church. It really is difficult to know who the Brethren
are!

In order to think clearly about this matter, and to
come to a positive conclusion, it will be necessary for
us to look at relevant scriptural teaching and practice,
and glance at appropriate historical evidence, before
facing head-on the question of Brethren identity
today.

2

WHAT DOES SCRIPTURE SAY?

One of our most vexing problems today is that the church on earth now functions in a way vastly different from that in which it functioned in New Testament days. Then it was—at least in a formal sense—one; now it is divided into a multitude of entities, each of which has a life and, in most cases, a unity of its own. Then it was in most cases small enough to be able to express its local unity with physical ease; now it is so large that in the majority of places it would hardly be possible for all believers to meet together, even if they were in a mind to do so. Then it was close in time to the historic events which had brought it into being; now it is far enough removed in time for long traditions to have firmly established their hold.

When we add to considerations like these the fact that we live in almost totally different cultural conditions, the sheer impossibility of reproducing the life of the New Testament church in every particular is clearly seen. Nevertheless, we are not left without adequate guidance. This study of the biblical material will address itself to four basic questions which it will attempt to answer with the help of that guidance:

1. Is there a comprehensive scriptural pattern for church life down the ages?

2. How does the New Testament regard the church?
3. What is the role of tradition?
4. Is there any difference of status between essential and non-essential matters?

Pattern or principles?

It is often maintained that Scripture provides a clear, precise and detailed pattern for church life. I vividly remember a discussion many years ago in the course of which the words, 'See that thou make all things according to the pattern shown thee in the mount' were quoted as if they settled the matter! The plain fact is that these words were spoken to Moses after God had revealed to him a detailed plan for the construction of the tabernacle in the wilderness. I have yet to discover a Gospel Hall built to these specifications!

This world may be 'a wilderness wide' (to quote one of J. N. Darby's hymns), but has God given to us in the New Testament a detailed plan for church life? If it should be maintained that he has, then the answer must be returned that it is a woefully inadequate one! For example, no instructions of any kind are given regarding the place where he is to be worshipped, the dress of the worshippers, the precise order of events that must take place, the duration of services etc. Very little is said about the way in which the initiatory rite and the sacred meal are to be conducted. For instance, no indication is given as to who should give thanks for the bread and wine.

It is the same with leadership in the church. Evidence regarding this is far from clear, hence it is not surprising that different views have been held on this subject—even among Brethren. Assuming that churches should always be led by elders and deacons (and this is not absolutely clear) no indication is given as to how the former (and probably also the latter) should be chosen. The contrast between Old and New Testaments could hardly be more stark.

But let us suppose that the New Testament *had* included a detailed pattern. In this case we would be under the obligation to jettison forthwith a number of activities carried on in our churches which are hallowed by long tradition. There is *no* direct scriptural warrant for such things as Sunday schools, women's meetings, young people's activities, gospel meetings—not to mention elders' meetings or even brothers' meetings.

There are good reasons why the New Testament did not include anything comparable with 'the pattern that was shown thee in the mount'. The *old* covenant was one of the *letter* in which things were spelled out in detail and meant to be applied literally. On the whole there was no room for initiative or innovation. In sharp contrast, the *new* covenant is one of the *Spirit*. While this does not exclude written commandments (the Spirit enables us to keep the letter) it does mean that there is a deeper dimension. The contrast should not be pressed too hard, but under the dispensation of the Spirit he gives guidance as to the ways in which the *principles* enunciated in the New Testament are to be applied in the ongoing life of the church.

Not only is the new covenant marked by an unprecedented diffusion of the Spirit; it is no longer confined to a single nation with its distinctive cultural patterns. It is a covenant with believing people of all nations throughout the rest of time.

If it had involved detailed regulations regarding church life and practice, these would necessarily have been given in terms of first-century customs. As a result the church would have been tied to these, worldwide, throughout the centuries. The Jews had

problems enough applying the detailed provisions of
old covenant law to the changing conditions of their
society. What a mercy that God did *not* lay down
detailed regulations but, instead, gave his Spirit to
guide the church in its application—and re-application
—of the timeless principles and guidelines of the New
Testament. For let no one be mistaken. God *has* given
guidance and continues to give it, though not in the
form of laws and statutes.

So, forms of worship, styles of leadership, methods of
evangelism, for example, are not intended to follow prescribed patterns but rather must express fundamental
principles like integrity, propriety and edification,
upon which the New Testament insists.

How does the New Testament regard the church?

Fundamental to a right appreciation of the New
Testament view of the church is insistence on its
unity. The church is one—Christ's body, his bride,
God's temple etc. Nothing that will be said subse-
quently should be taken to imply disregard for the
importance of this basic assertion. There is only one
church in the New Testament, and we are bound to do
everything in our power to bear witness to this fact,
not only by word but also by action.

Having said that, it has often been pointed out that
the word *ekklesia* (church) is used with reference not
only to all God's people everywhere and at all times,
but also to a local congregation. With a single
exception, the word is used (in the singular) in no
other sense. The church, incidentally, in its universal
sense is not the aggregate of all local churches, but a
local church is a manifestation of the universal
church. It is, so to speak, a microcosm of the whole.

Those of us in the Open Brethren tradition need to

be reminded that local churches in New Testament times, though self-governing, were not totally independent. Rather, they were interdependent. Their sense of belonging together was a lively one which found expression in a number of ways.

1. *Intercommunion*
They practised what has come to be called intercommunion. Individuals in good standing in one church were welcomed by others—assuming that Paul's recommendation of individuals like Phoebe (*Rom. 16:1–2*), Epaphroditus (*Phil. 2:29*) and Mark (*Col. 4:10*) was acted upon and they were 'received'. Reception, it should be noted, involved a good deal more than admission to church services. To 'receive' someone (*Phil. 2:29*) implied loving concern and tender care. Paul specifically requested the church in Rome to help Phoebe 'in whatever way she may require from you' (*Rom. 16:2*).

2. *Interchange of ministry*
Since Paul's letters come from a period of pioneer missionary activity, it may be a little unwise to generalize too much, but it is worth noting that it was not only Christians on the move for personal or business reasons who were to be received, but also those who were engaged in itinerant Christian service. Not only Paul himself but his numerous helpers moved easily from place to place. If Jews visiting a synagogue were invited to share in spoken ministry (*Acts 13:15*) surely Christian believers would have been afforded a similar privilege. The evidence does not suggest that the interchange of personnel reached anything like the proportions it has reached among Brethren today, but it was certainly practised.

3. *Inter-communication*
Paul's request that the churches at Colosse and Laod-
icea should share the letters they had received from
him (*Col. 4:15–16*) shows that inter-communication as
well as inter-communion was the order of the day. The
practice continued, and there is plenty of evidence
from post-apostolic times to show that churches maintained contact with each other by means of correspon-
dence. They exchanged information, offered advice—
and even reproof—and encouraged each other in this
way.

4. *Inter-church aid*
The concern shown by the churches for each other
went beyond the interchange of personnel and corres-
pondence. The church in Antioch provided material
aid for the Jerusalem church in time of famine (*Acts
11:27–30*) and Paul went to very considerable lengths
to encourage the churches in Galatia, Macedonia and
Achaia to do the same.

5. *Joint consultation*
It was surely the path of wisdom for the churches in
Jerusalem and Antioch to attempt to repair their
damaged relationship by means of a joint consultation
(*Acts 15:1ff.*). That the attempt was not crowned by
lasting success need not obscure the wisdom of joint
consultation on matters of common interest, especially
when there is a background of disagreement and
friction. It is surely to be regretted that (correct)
insistence on local autonomy has sometimes served as
a bar to consultation between churches when this
might have been to mutual advantage.

We must now return to the single instance where
the word 'church' is used in a third sense. *Acts 9:31*

informs us that 'the church throughout Judea, Galilee and Samaria enjoyed a time of peace'. Here the word means neither the universal church (for surely we should deduce from *Acts 11:19* that churches had been formed in other areas than these), nor, very clearly, a local church! The church 'throughout Judea, Galilee and Samaria' would almost certainly have been composed of Jewish believers. Basically, it was the Jerusalem church in dispersion, and it would have roughly corresponded with what Paul calls 'God's churches in Judea which are in Christ Jesus' (*Gal. 1:22*). It begins to look as though *Acts 9:31* is describing a number of churches that possess common features—origin and ethnic character—in terms of a single identity.

There is also the fact that the term, 'church', is used for a 'house church' that was actually part of a city church. For example, it is clear from *Romans 16* that there were a number of house churches (see especially *v.5*, but also *vv.10, 11, 14, 15*). It is true that Paul does not address his letter to 'the church' in Rome, but to 'all in Rome who are loved by God and called to be saints' (*Rom. 1:7*). Yet there is no evidence—but rather the contrary—that the church in Rome ever regarded itself as more than one. It looks as if the one church in Rome comprised a number of house churches. (And the time was to come when the church in many a large city would consist of a number of 'parish' churches, *yet still regard itself as one*.)

Admittedly using the term in the plural, Paul refers to 'the Galatian churches' (*1 Cor. 16:1*), 'the churches in the province of Asia' (*1 Cor. 16:19*) and 'the churches of Judea' (*Gal. 1:22*). Without prejudice to their local autonomy and individual identity, Paul is prepared to distinguish them from churches in other provinces and areas or of different ethnic character. In however limited a sense, they have an identity of their own.

Most instructive is Paul's use of the term 'churches of the Gentiles' (*Rom. 16:4*). Paul was the apostle to the Gentiles. It was his preaching to them which provoked into action the Judaisers of *Romans 15:1* and *Galatians 1:7*. The churches of the Gentiles had an identity of their own not merely on ethnic grounds but also on religious ones, since Gentile believers were drawn from those who, prior to their conversion, had been 'excluded from citizenship in Israel and foreigners to the covenants of the promise, without hope and without God in the world' (*Eph. 2:12*).

Paul was keenly aware of the unity in Christ of converted Gentiles and Jews. *Ephesians 2* leaves no possibility for doubting that. But he was also aware of the common features possessed by Gentile believers on the one hand and Jewish believers on the other, which might have contributed towards a breach of fellowship. Without doubt, one of the major reasons why he promoted the 'collection for God's people' (*1 Cor. 16:1*), and took the proceeds to Judea in person (with Gentile representatives) at the risk of his life, was to demonstrate the solidarity of Jews and Gentiles in Christ.

In short, it begins to look as if the term 'church' may be used in the New Testament (usually, but not always, in the plural) to denominate a group of churches which have common features not possessed by all the churches. Geographical situation (as in the case of a number of house churches in the same city or a number of churches in a province), ethnic origin (notable Jewish or Gentile) or religious background (overlapping with the former distinction between Jew and Gentile) justify such a use of the term.

What is the role of tradition?

The term 'tradition', used of the act of passing on something of value from one to another, and also of the content of what is passed on, is to be found in the New Testament.

Paul praised the Corinthians for holding to the traditions (teachings, NIV) which he had passed on to them (*1 Cor. 11:2*) and urged Timothy to entrust to reliable men who were qualified to teach them to others, the things which he had taught him (*2 Tim. 2:2*). These traditions clearly include the gospel message (*1 Cor. 15:1ff.*) and the account of the institution of the Lord's Supper (*1 Cor. 11:23*), and as far as we are concerned extend to the whole of the New Testament (and the Old as well, for that matter). Clearly, they are not to be added to.

There is another kind of tradition altogether, ruthlessly exposed by Jesus for the worthless thing it is. This he refers to as the tradition of the elders. Basically, it represents an attempt to adapt the unchanging law given to Moses to a changing world *and make it equally binding*.

The grounds on which Jesus condemned this kind of tradition are as follows:

1. It nullifies the word of God (*Mt. 15:6*), since it enables men to evade clear commands of God with impunity (*Mt. 15:3–6*).
2. It focuses attention on the external, ceremonial aspects of religion, to the neglect of its more important, internal, moral aspects (*Mt. 15:16–20; 23:23–24*).
3. It makes for inhumanity and neglect of obligations towards other people (*Mt. 13:4–5*).
4. It leads inexorably to hypocrisy and double-think (*Mt. 23:16–22; 27–31*).

A moment's thought will reveal that Brethren are not without this second kind of tradition (as well as the first). It falls foul of each of Christ's condemnations in ways like this (taking them one by one):

1. Insistence on 'ritual' preaching of the gospel at a gospel meeting attended only (or even mainly) by converted people constitutes an evasion of the clear command to preach the gospel to the world of unbelievers.

2. Rigid enforcement of the wearing of headcovering by worshipping women may be accompanied by bitter feelings, harsh words and unloving actions.

3. Turning away from religious services young people (in particular) whose dress is judged unsuitable for the occasion, not to mention the harm done to women presenting themselves for worship without the prescribed headcovering.

4. The subtle distinctions drawn and devices used to enable women to address men in public without appearing to do so (*e.g.* the use of tape-recorded addresses and even the device of men sitting behind a screen in order to listen to a woman missionary giving her report without appearing to do so).

We would do well to distinguish valid tradition from that which is phoney.

Is there any difference of status between things that are essential and those that are non-essential?

One of the surprises of New Testament study is the discovery that Paul, who could be so inflexible and dogmatic, could also be yielding and sensitive to the extent of resorting to what appears to be compromise. His phrase about becoming 'all things to all men' may have been terribly abused, but it was of vital importance to him. He was prepared to become 'like a Jew' and 'like one under the law' and yet he was also willing to act 'like one not having the law'. He was even prepared to become 'weak' (in conscience) for the sake of the gospel (*1 Cor. 9:19–23*).

The example most pertinent to us is Paul's attitude towards circumcision. Paul knew that circumcision was neither here nor there (*Gal. 6:15*). This meant that in one set of circumstances he was prepared to apply it (to Timothy, *Acts 16:3*) whereas in a totally different context he resolutely refused to countenance it (in the case of Titus, *Gal. 2:3–5*).

One of the most difficult tasks facing Brethren today is to decide what 'means anything' (Paul's actual phrase in *Gal. 6:15*). Too often we have taken issue with people over matters which—in the circumstances—are not of fundamental importance. The following principles may serve as rough guides:

1. Issues of fundamental importance are likely to be *clearly* revealed in Scripture. Thus the personal return of Jesus Christ is essential: whether it will take place in two stages, or occur before or after the millennium, is not essential—these are matters not clearly revealed.
2. A parallel guideline is that an issue of fundamental importance is unlikely to have been denied by any significant number of genuine believers at any time in the history of the church.
3. A circumstantial consideration is that a matter which is not in itself essential (like circumcision) may become such if it *clearly* undermines a doctrine that *is* essential. This guideline requires careful handling for it may appear to *me* that infant baptism (to take a modern example) undermines the doctrine of justification by faith alone. But if some-

one like Martin Luther could believe in both, then I must be careful not to project my conscience in the matter on to another believer.

The somewhat radical conclusion that follows from this is that few, if any, distinctive Brethren beliefs and practices lie in the area of essentials (nor, for that matter, do the issues that divide Brethren from each other). Their ecclesiastical separation from other believers rests on other ground which we must examine in the next section.

3

WHAT DOES HISTORY TELL US?

It will help us in our search for Brethren identity if we look at our history. We will ask—and attempt to answer—four questions:

1. What was the essence of the initial Brethren position?
2. Did the early Brethren tolerate diversity?
3. Has the Brethren movement changed down the years?
4. Is it monochrome around the world today?

What was the essence of the initial Brethren position?

There would be some excuse if we were to come to the conclusion that the Brethren movement commenced with a fundamentally negative view of things. The Roman Catholic church was beyond the pale. The established church was partner in an unholy alliance with the state, and seemed to regard every baptised parishioner—whatever the state of his beliefs and morals—as a brother in Christ (witness the burial service). The various nonconformist churches held a more or less sectarian position based on their distinctive beliefs and practices. And every existing church—which claimed the name—drew an unscriptural distinction between clergy and laity.

31

From the way in which its leading men wrote, one might also be forgiven for imagining that the Brethren movement began at a time of spiritual decline and religious apostasy. But this is very far from being the case. A momentous spiritual revival had taken place bringing into existence a new group of churches— Wesleyan Methodists of varying hues—which had succeeded to a limited but not insignificant extent in evangelizing the new industrialized working classes. What is more, the sparks of life within the eighteenth-century Church of England had been fanned into a flame, with increasing numbers of evangelical clergymen preaching the gospel to some effect. Even the old dissenting churches which had largely succumbed to the rationalism and heresies of the eighteenth century were springing into new and vigorous life. (An observant visitor to many an English village will find a chapel built in the 1820s.)

The fact is that, just as revolutions tend to occur when things are getting better, so the Brethren 'revolution' began at a time when the spiritual tide was running higher than for a long time—but not high enough for ardent, young spirits.

We should be following an equally misleading trail if we were to seek for the essence of the Brethren movement in the quest for Christian unity. That this was one of the concerns closest to its heart is beyond question. The divided state of the church was a great grief to Brethren. But it was also a great grief to others, such as Edward Irving and the leaders of the Catholic Apostolic church who cannot by any stretch of the imagination be designated Brethren.

Similarly, the concern for evangelism which was so marked a feature of the Brethren movement in its early day was not distinctive. We have already commented on the evangelistic fervour of the Methodists—which was not as marked in the 1820s and '30s as it had been, but was still keen—and of the Baptists and Congregationalists. As for the Anglicans, they may have become more discreet in their evangelistic presentations at home, but they—like the other denominations—were becoming very active in foreign missions.

We shall not go very far astray if we come to the conclusion that the thing above everything else which distinguished the early Brethren was the absolute priority which they accorded to the Word of God. Evidence for the truth of this statement is not far to find.

What other new religious movement devoted itself so extensively, from its very beginning, to the study, exposition and application of the Scriptures? Its literature consisted of little else than biblical exposition. Its most *characteristic* religious activity was not the 'breaking of Bread' meeting (though the form that this took was somewhat characteristic) but the 'Bible reading'. Not infrequently, in those early days, the 'reading' was based on the Bible in the original languages.

One of the earliest leaders of the movement—G. V. Wigram—financed the massive task, in those days, of compiling the Englishman's Concordances to the Greek of the New Testament and the Hebrew and Aramaic of the Old. An early, if transient, adherent— S. P. Tregelles—edited one of the three great critical texts of the Greek New Testament produced in the nineteenth century.

But perhaps the clearest evidence of the importance attached by the early Brethren to Scripture is the somewhat bizarre article in *The Christian Witness* which sets out a complete system of Canon Law, using the words of Scripture alone. The article is clearly a 'take off', not intended to be taken seriously as a blueprint for church life, but it is an eloquent assertion of the claim that Scripture is the only normative basis.

It may be objected that this is no more than the Reformation principle of *Sola Scriptura* which was also avowed by contemporary evangelicals as their lode star. But, just as Anabaptists of the sixteenth century chided the Reformers with failure to be sufficiently radical in their application of Scripture to the problems of the church in their day, so nineteenth-century Brethren belaboured contemporary evangelicals for their failure to be consistent biblicists.

Here, if anywhere, is the essential principle of the Brethren. For man-made tradition they cared not a hoot: Scripture, on the other hand, was the voice of God.

Did the early Brethren tolerate diversity?

At first sight, a negative answer to this question seems to be demanded. Why else were the disagreements among them attended by such bitter and protracted controversies?

But closer examination reveals that, even among those who followed Darby, a certain amount of diversity was tolerated. For example, differences of opinion and practice regarding baptism failed to sour the relationships between those, like Wigram, who held to believers' baptism and those, like Darby, who defended household baptism with biblical arguments remarkably similar to those used by evangelical Anglicans! As for those from whom Darby separated himself (and his followers), they were able to contain disagreements in a variety of areas. Though the majority adhered to Darby's theory of a Secret Rapture of the church prior to the Great Tribulation, men like Müller, Craik and Chapman did not toe the party line, and suffered little hostility as a result. Leadership patterns varied considerably; there was no uniform terminology for naming meeting places; the Bethesda churches in the West Country practised a semi-connexionalism that was foreign to Brethren in other parts of the country. Other regional variations may be detected, such as the practice in some parts of the country, but not in others, of different men giving thanks for the bread and the wine in communion services. There also seem to have been some variations in the role of sisters in church life.

Has the Brethren movement changed down the years?

Some people seem to imagine that the traditional way of doing things has been handed down unchanged from the Brethren 'fathers' of the early nineteenth century. This is very far from being the case. I suspect that, if Darby, Müller and Groves, for example, were to come back among us they would each be surprised beyond measure at some of the things they found going on!

Let us look at some of the changes that have taken place, confining ourselves for the most part to those which have gained acceptance right across the (Open) Brethren board, though noting in parenthesis a few of those which have been accepted less generally.

At the level of theology, the earliest Brethren were Calvinists to a man. In the process of time they adopted the dispensationalist approach to Scripture (which was largely the brain-child of J. N. Darby) and greatly modified their Calvinism. Eventually, it became little more than a memory, maintained by a few, rediscovered by some, but largely a thing of the past.

Now, however, it is increasingly common to find people who are dubious about some aspects of dispensationalism. The idea of a two-stage Second Advent, with a Secret Rapture of the saints, followed by a period of seven years of tribulation for the Jews, at the end of which Christ will return with the saints to set up an earthly kingdom of a Jewish character seems to be losing credibility.

When we look at the ecclesiastical practice of Brethren down the years, we find even clearer evidence of change. The use of musical instruments is a case in point. There are probably few, if any, assemblies in England where they are never used. It seems that they have been introduced gradually, over the years, first in gospel meetings, then at mid-week meetings, and in a smaller but growing number of cases for services of worship.

Another example is the demise of the open platform. At one time it was a common practice to arrange meetings, and even conferences, without inviting speakers, leaving it to the Lord to move the hearts of suitable speakers to be present and to come forward to speak. This practice has been greatly modified. (I recall being invited, some years ago, to be *present* at such an open conference.) Now it has largely died out.

Fairly widespread has been the introduction of modern methods of youth work incorporating various kinds of physical recreations and cultural pursuits. Holiday camps for children and young people have become quite general.

Within the worshipping life of the church, the practice of allocating a period of time after the breaking of bread for ministry of the Word (thus abrogating the rigid separation between worship, ministry, prayer and evangelism so characteristic of most Brethren in earlier days) has spread. In some instances it takes place at the beginning of the service, as preparation for worship. Occasionally, the service is structured (though almost always there is a period of open worship).

Traditional practice with regard to conferences has been modified over and above the decline of the open platform. The pattern of an annual Saturday conference with two addresses before tea and two after has been modified in half a dozen different ways, or even discontinued.

As it happens, this is being written on Christmas Day, and I am reminded that Brethren attitudes towards the observance of the Christian Year have changed very considerably. Instead of regarding Christmas as a pagan festival devoid of Christian significance, most Brethren accept it as a somewhat artificial but nevertheless useful reminder of the incarnation of Christ. (What would the early Brethren have said about religious services on Christmas morning?) The extent to which other events in the Christian Year are celebrated varies from church to church. But there can be no question that a fairly general revision of earlier attitudes has taken place on this issue, as on so many others.

None is more suprising than the changes in behaviour and lifestyle. Initially, Brethren sat loose to material possessions, adopted a negative attitude towards society and politics (with few exceptions) and followed a generally anti-establishment attitude (in the non-religious as well as in the religious sphere!). Nowadays, Brethren have a not altogether undeserved reputation for being well-heeled, living in above-average quality housing and driving expensive cars. The proportion of Brethren voting in elections must have increased quite considerably, and, while many Brethren registered as conscientious objectors during the last war, a considerable number joined the forces, some of them attaining high rank.

These more or less general changes in belief, practices and attitudes put into context the more dramatic changes referred to in the opening part of this booklet, and show that they differ in degree rather than in kind. Flexibility and adaptability, rather than rigidity, are authentic characteristics of the Brethren movement. In proof of this, the movement has been able to contain within its ranks a number of men of independent judgement who have held distinctive views on a number of non-essential matters. One thinks, for instance, of G. H. Lang and H. L. Ellison.

Is the Brethren movement monochrome around the world?

We have seen that the essential feature of the Brethren movement is its total submission to Scripture, that its beliefs and practices have never been uniform and have changed in varying degrees down the years. It remains to look briefly at the situation around the world to see whether the same is true outside Britain.

The impression that may be gained from missionary reports is that Brethren churches are the same the world over. But this is very far from the truth. Missionaries reporting to their supporting churches naturally tend to draw attention only to those features of church life overseas that are similar to those at home. And to a great extent, we who listen to their reports tend to *assume* that things are the same.

It comes as something of a surprise, therefore, to realize that the Brethren movement worldwide is characterized by even greater variation and flexibility than is the case at home. A few examples will suffice to establish the point. The elements used in the Lord's Supper may be not bread and wine, but items of staple diet that are more appropriate to the local culture. Worship may be more structured than is normally the case here. Women may play a greater part in worship

than we are used to. Missionaries, and sometimes
nationals, exercise a full-time local ministry that is
more common than was the case here, until recently.
Local churches may be less isolated and form part of a
semi-connexional system in a way that is unusual in
Britain.

Here then, as in Brethren history and biblical
precedents, we find something very different from
monolithic adherence to a pattern fixed for all time
and every place.

4

THINGS THAT MATTER TODAY

Let us start this section by surveying the ground we have already covered. We began by introducing the subject in a general way, and suggested a number of reasons why it can be said that the Brethren are facing an identity crisis. We then turned to the all-important biblical study in the course of which a number of claims were made. First, that the New Testament does not provide a detailed blue-print for the conduct of church life; second, that the New Testament does provide slender, but significant, evidence showing that it is not improper for a number of churches having a common origin, a common geographical location or a common ethnic origin, to feel a sense of belonging together; third, that, though there is a form of tradition that must be handed down intact from generation to generation, there is another kind that is reprehensible and should be jettisoned; finally that, whereas some things are essential and should never be changed, others are non-essential and therefore variable.

Turning from biblical to historical evidence, it was maintained that the essential and characteristic thing about our Brethren founding-fathers was their insistence on the supreme and unqualified authority of Scripture; that, far from insisting on rigid conformity to a detailed pattern of belief and practice, the early

Brethren tolerated a fair degree of diversity; that, in place of a rigid pattern handed down unchanged from one generation to another, Brethren beliefs and ways of doing things have changed quite substantially down the years; and that there is similar variation in Brethren patterns around the world today.

Now we must draw the threads together and relate them to the current scene. The question of Brethren identity *does* matter and is one that demands urgent attention, particularly in view of the new surges of spiritual life that are manifesting themselves around the country. The reasons why this is so are numerous. They include:

1. Realism
2. Responsibility
3. Scripture
4. Practicality

Realism

To pretend that the Brethren do not form a recognizable feature of the ecclesiastical landscape is to fly in face of the facts. Ostrich-like, we may persuade ourselves that we do not exist, but outside observers have no difficulty in discerning us!

Though we have no denominational structures as such, we nevertheless possess powerful infrastructures which bestow a kind of corporate identity upon us, whether we like it or not. Any movement is held together by printed organs. The Brethren have their magazines and other publications which may circulate to some extent outside the membership but which are nevertheless primarily—if not solely—*intended* to create something of a common mind among us. (This booklet was originally written as a series of articles in HARVESTER, a Brethren magazine!) The magazines in question have as their subject-matter biblical exposition (usually of a fairly distinctive nature), feature articles on matters of common interest to those within the movement, and news concerned almost entirely with events taking place within Brethren circles.

One magazine is concerned exclusively with missionary matters, not of an interdenominational character but relating almost exclusively to the activities of missionaries sent out by Brethren churches—assuming, that is, that they have complied with procedures determined by its editors.

A number of publishing houses serve the peculiar needs of the family of churches we are concerned with (though not always exclusively so). One of them used to publish a list of the addresses of those churches. Though it possessed no 'official' status, it served as a means of (very roughly) identifying the churches which regard themselves as part of a group of related churches.

Conferences perform a similar function of expressing and fostering a sense of common identity. These conferences assume different forms, including day conferences, weekend ones, residential or non-residential events, held annually, monthly or at other intervals. The use of itinerant rather than local speakers at such conferences, as at normal church meetings, acts powerfully towards the same end.

Above all, perhaps, those churches which teach a strict doctrine of 'separation' (from other believers, as well as from 'the world') foster thereby a very strong sense of identity. How can such teaching do anything else?

Incidentally, but importantly, these same mechanisms undergird the polarization within the Brethren movement referred to in the first section of this booklet. Some churches are known by the magazines they circulate, the conferences they arrange, the speakers they engage, the missionary agencies they use, and their teaching on separation.

Those churches which are beginning to distance themselves from the Brethren scene may assert that they are no longer part of it. Without doubt that point may be reached. But before it is, such churches would do well to weigh other elements in the situation, such as those which follow.

Responsibility

One of the most intractable elements in human existence is history. It is something which *cannot* be altered, try as we may, nor is it easy to escape its consequences. And it certainly imposes obligations upon us.

Reformers like Martin Luther, though disagreeing with many aspects of the church in which they had been brought up, strove long and hard to bring the blessings of reform to others within that church. Similarly, we who are the product of historical development, who have links of fellowship and association with a particular circle of churches and have received much from the connection, have a responsibility to do all in our power to contribute to their welfare.

This responsibility, it must be stressed, need not and should not be in competition with our responsibility towards other churches outside our immediate circle. No one in his right mind denies that he has a duty to love the members of his immediate family circle on the ground that it would deflect him from loving his neighbour in the wider sense. Responsibilities at various levels may come into conflict with each other, but conflicts of this sort are to be resolved not by

denying that one or other of them is valid, but by
balancing one against the other.

Scripture

The decisive consideration is the scriptural one which,
as we have already seen, is the nub of the whole
matter. It is here that the buck stops. Brethren
tradition, as such, counts for little or nothing. Like any
other form of non-scriptural tradition, it must never be
accorded a share in the sovereignty of Scripture. It
may need to be taken into consideration, particularly
in formulating a policy for the application of scriptural
teaching which takes into account the consciences of
'weaker' brethren, but it must never be allowed to
acquire normative force.

Over against some traditional forms of Brethrenism
which speak as if Brethren churches were the only
valid form of corporate Christianity and therefore see
no need to come to terms with the existence of other
forms of church life apart from their own, we must
affirm that times have changed since the New Testament was written! The formal unity of the one, true
church which was no more than endangered in those
days has been shattered—probably beyond hope of
repair. Yet the New Testament is not without guidance
for us in such a sad situation.

For, as we have seen, there were churches in New
Testament times that possessed distinctive features
(theological as well as racial or geographical) and yet
recognized churches that were different from them.
They gave expression to their underlying unity with
churches that differed from them as well as those that
did not. Far from holding themselves aloof from other
types of church (if Paul's concern for fellowship with
Jewish churches is anything to go by) they went to

great lengths to demonstrate their unity in Christ.

Over against the open-ended Brethren position which tends to sit loose to responsibility towards churches of a *similar* type, we must point to the evidence within the New Testament for the existence of groupings of churches (within a city, within a region, or with a similar ethnic or theological background) which had some kind of corporate identity of their own *in addition to* their overall identity within the total circle of Christian churches.

Practicality

That it is practicable to work on such a basis in the changed conditions of the post-apostolic age is clearly demonstrated by the example of men like George Müller of Bristol. It is almost impossible to dispute the *bona fides* of Müller as an authentic leader of the Brethren (though Exclusive Brethren have attempted to do so!). Bethesda, Bristol, had its distinctive features (but we have already made the point that Brethren identity is not dependent on total adherence to any man-made list of requirements) and exercised a remarkable influence on the development of the Brethren movement in the West Country and beyond. Yet Müller was able to combine this with remarkable openness to other Christians and other churches. He preached in other churches, and ministers of other churches preached in Bethesda. His Scripture Knowledge Institute channelled financial aid and stimulated prayer support on behalf of missionaries not only from Brethren churches but from others also (admittedly, provided that they operated on lines that Müller felt to be compatible with scriptural teaching!). Late in life, his worldwide preaching tours took on something of an ecumenical character. In his case, at least, a strong sense of identity with (Open) Brethren was not incompatible with biblical catholicity.

Nor need it be so for others. Today, many of us are committed to a Brethren position, as outlined above, in terms of freedom to apply the teaching of Scripture to contemporary situations without rigid constraints from any other source—including Brethren tradition. At the same time, we feel perfectly free to fellowship with and minister to Christians and churches which are not so committed.

The two positions are not incompatible. Indeed, the second is required by the first. Clear scriptural teaching requires that we submit not only to the constraints placed upon us by fellowship with like-minded believers but also to those which arise from our fellowship with all who are 'in Christ'. If, as Brethren, we are committed to the principle of 'Scripture alone', then we really have no choice in the matter.

Conclusion

An analogy may help. In the global village in which we live—or is it a global city?—we must all be keenly aware of our responsibilities to our fellow-men. Whether they be victims of famine in Ethiopia, of racism in South Africa, or of economic and political tensions in Central America, we feel a sense of responsibility towards them as fellow human beings.

But that should not deter us from feeling a special sense of responsibility towards fellow-nationals, fellow-townsmen or members of our own family. It may be true that nationalism and chauvinism of any kind can become terrible masters. (Patriotism is most definitely 'not enough'.) But, kept firmly in check, these lesser loyalties have their claim upon us.

In a somewhat similar way, loyalty towards the Christian community in its widest, universal sense, should not exclude lesser loyalties. In particular, we have a somewhat distinctive duty towards those with whom we have special ties resulting from a shared history, joint associations and (more or less) common convictions.

That is not to say that we should be aiming at total uniformity. Not at all. We have seen that, historically and around the world today, true Brethren likeness is to be seen, not in outward conformity to a man-made list of beliefs and practices, but in inward submission to the requirements of Scripture.

While in practice there is likely to be a good deal of uniformity—certainly in matters of fundamental importance where one should expect that uniformity to be total—a great deal of diversity in secondary matters is fully compatible with the master-principle of Brethren conviction—the absolute supremacy of Scripture.

The fact that this is not the sole prerogative of those known as Brethren might be thought to make it inappropriate as a defining principle. On the contrary, it is eminently appropriate. For it is the reason why Brethren have arrived at their most distinctive practices, and it is the reason why they could go from strength to strength if only they continue to be guided by Scripture alone. It is open to question whether any other Christian body has been as radical as the early Brethren in following the teaching of Scripture regardless of tradition. (Some, such as certain Anabaptists groups, might be judged to be close seconds or even to have outrun us.)

The blurring of the distinction between Brethren and other evangelicals nowadays has taken place because *they* have become more consistent in their profession of submission to Scripture. As a result they are moving much closer to *us*! Long may that movement continue, and, to change the figure slightly, may we not be outrun by them in the move towards Scripture which has been bringing us together.

The Brethren never did want a distinctive name. Let us who have been given the name live in accordance with it as we move forward together into an era in which, please God, the distinction between Brethren and brethren will mean less and less.

The way will not be easy. Pitfalls abound. It would be much easier to retreat into an unreal spiritual world of make-belief. There will be many things to hold in balance. We will need to avoid narrow exclusiveness on the one hand, and woolly comprehensiveness on the other. We must avoid foolish attempts to create rigid denominational structures, while being careful to foster links of fellowship and service ministries for those with whom we have so much in common. And in our eagerness to avoid all these dangers we must steer clear of yet another—that of distancing ourselves from all other churches so that we end up in that unscriptural position, a local church standing alone without real links with any other church. For if there is no such thing in the New Testament as an isolated Christian, neither is there such a misshapen thing as a solitary local church.